ONE IN A MILLION

poetry today

One In A Million

Edited by Suzy Walton

First published in Great Britain in 2001 by Poetry Today, an imprint of
Penhaligon Page Ltd, Remus House, Coltsfoot Drive, Woodston, Peterborough. PE2 9JX

A Catalogue record for this book is available from the British Library

ISBN 1 86226 653 0

Typesetting and layout, Penhaligon Page Ltd, England.
Printed and bound by Forward Press Ltd, England

Foreword

One In A Million is a compilation of poetry, featuring some of our finest poets. This book gives an insight into the essence of modern living and deals with the reality of life today. We think we have created an anthology with a universal appeal.

There are many technical aspects to the writing of poetry and *One In A Million* contains free verse and examples of more structured work from a wealth of talented poets.

Poetry is a coat of many colours. Today's poets write in a limitless array of styles: traditional rhyming poetry is as alive and kicking today as modern free verse. Language ranges from easily accessible to intricate and elusive.

Poems have a lot to offer in our fast-paced 'instant' world. Reading poems gives us an opportunity to sit back and explore ourselves and the world around us.

Contents

A Special Poem For A Very Special Friend

Through memories I look, some old and some new
No matter what I have ever been through
When I've needed you the most, you have always been there
You are the one true person who really cares
So as a token of gratitude and my love
I write this small poem just for you, my peaceful dove

If you ever need a friend to lend an ear
You're never alone I will always be near
If you ever begin to feel sad and low, in total despair
You have to know I will always be there

We have been friends for nearly seven years to this date
I can't remember a time when you haven't been a good mate
We have seen each other through the good and the bad
I can't remember us ever being upset when together, not even mad

Though we don't see each other all that much
We still try our hardest to keep in touch
Now we are older leading a separate life
We try to chat even if it's just to talk about strife!

Never forget no matter how or when, I am always here for you
I know I can always expect the same from you too.
Now my little poem must come to an end
Dedicated to you Samantha, my bestest ever friend

Love you lots forever and always in friendship

From your ever faithful bud,

Louise Ann Beevers

Sweet Damage

Just friends never works
We've tried it and failed
The lid on our lust
Wasn't quite so tightly nailed.

Just friends as a concept
Is fundamentally flawed
There's warmth in our kiss
As our lips slowly thawed.

Just friends is no solution
Your grip is far too tight
I want you to let go
But stay another night.

Just friends is nice
But isn't quite as fun
And as you pull me closer
There's sweet damage to be done.

Jo Forbes

Last Moments

Her voice is the soft rhythmic hum
Of her engines, hypnotic,
Strangely comforting. She speaks to me
And responds to my touch
As deep in her heart, I steer her course
'Hand steady Jack, steer her true.'

Above me and around
Her people stand to, expectant
Each ready, aye ready. She waits with me
And occasionally sighs
'10 degrees starboard.' '10 degrees starboard on sir.'
'Keep steady Jack, keep her true.'

The klaxon sounds,
Our guns open up, pounding.
Each thud sends vibrations down through her decks
Like hammer blows
'Attack imminent, state red, hard over.' 'Hard over sir.'
'Heave that wheel Jack, bring us through.'

A terrific crash, she heels over sharply
Her hull jolts, shudders.
We plunge into darkness as her life-force ebbs.
'Wheelhouse to bridge?' No reply. 'Wheelhouse to bridge sir?'
'Time to leave Jack, we are doomed.'

Suffocating black smoke, eyes streaming
Lungs choking.
I make for the upper deck, numb and shaking.
Through bleeding ears, I hear her groan
And know she is dying.
'Goodbye Jack, your heart of oak is true.'

Brent William Beckett

To My Best Friend

We two go back in time so many years,
To school days, learning more than we were taught
Of boys and love and adolescent fears
That surfaced with the knowledge that we sought.
When gradually we went our separate ways
To share our lives with other company,
We knew within our hearts that all our days
We'd stay the constant friends we used to be.
Though times are few when we can get together
And remember all the moments we have shared,
Those memories will stay with us forever
Because of all the special ways we've cared.

Irene Thompson

Second Chance

I had a special friend whom I often considered a pain
Emotionally she could be such a drain
Whenever you spoke to her she was full of doom and gloom
Whenever she was present a black cloud was in the room

I tried to help her through her turmoil
I tried to help her through her pain
But no matter what I said or did
The attempts were all in vain.

It's hard to understand depression, I have a zest for life
Yet I have lost someone so special that it cuts me like a knife

I had a special friend who I hold so dear
Why she took her life, to me will never be clear
I just wish that I could have held her near
In the hope that she still would be here

U Hanley

In Memory Of A Friend And Mother

And yet, it is the simpleness of things
That I remember
You ~ always there to listen
Always my defender

And you ~ always there with a caring hand
To wipe away a tear
To smite a crushing snub
To snuff a gnawing fear

Dear you ~ always there with a cup of tea
And friendly word
The one that I would heed
The one that I preferred

So is it any wonder now, this life
You've quietly left
I laid my lonely head
Upon your pillow and wept

Helen Rowena Jackson

Friendship

Friendship is very important even more so at school
If you have a good friend you can tell them anything and it won't go any further
If you are unlucky and tell your friend your darkest secrets they could tell the world.
I feel I have found a good friend called Anouska
I can tell her anything
I am very lucky to have found such a good friend.
She has introduced me to new people
She doesn't mind when I moan
She is there for me.

Francesca Elliott

Friends Forever

A friend is a person
who is always there.
When times are bad
they show they care.
Through thick and thin
they stand by you
they help you with
the things you do.
It's hard to find
a real true friend
who'll see things through
until the end.
A special person
that you have found
you pick up the phone
they come right round.
A friendship that should
always be
though there are times
you disagree.
I'll miss you dearly
you were my best friend,
it was hard for you
towards the end.
But I know you're there
watching over me.
And my best friend
you will always be.

P Richardson

She's left us a legacy for all to share,
Her two young boys to remember in prayer,
Our future King and Prince Harry so dear,
Will carry her love to pass on through the years.

You were the Princess, England's dream,
The Queen of Hearts for all to see,
But now you're an angel high above,
Filled with sparkle and with love.

It's time to say our goodbyes to you,
Our hands reunited through and through,
The World all over, tears will fall,
For a beautiful rose that was plucked from us all.

E Butler

A Special Friend

Betty is her name,
An old school pal.
We shared a game,
Playing rounders in the lane.

She resided in Mount Pleasant
With steps up to the door.
I waited while Betty freshened,
Before approaching me across the floor!

At school we sat together,
Not writing with a feather.
Then, when playtime came
We joined in games.

School teacher's books we carried
In those carefree happy days!
As time went by we both married
And went our separate ways.

Some years later at Oakdale,
An avenue where we both resided
Until that is ~ the house went up 'for sale'
And we moved, once again our paths divided.

June Maughan

Friendship

For years now you have been my greatest friend
With your trust and support until the end.
Now by death we have been torn apart,
I am devastated ~ broken is my heart.
That you have gone forever I can't bear to think
Our chain of love is broken ~ I'm left with the missing link,
I am filled with this deep emotion we call grief,
The pain it brings beyond belief.
Greater than mere sorrow it's difficult to describe it.
Sheer and utter desolation is how I would define it.
And oft times the smile upon my face belies
This torment that in my whole body lies.
Each morning I awake, before me a picture of you and I
And a ceaseless yearning of happy days gone by.
Hoping always tomorrow will be better than today,
That this awful emptiness will go away.
But knowing tonight when the world's asleep I'll weep,
Slowly time will pass, fond memories of you linger on
Recalled by a gesture ~ words of a familiar song,
A word from someone meant sincerely to be kind
Brings quite a different reaction I soon find
As upon my cheek tears begin to fall again,
Will there ever be an end to this remorse ~ this pain.

As my confidant, my friend you were loyal and so true.
Whate'er befell I could always rely on you.
In time life will get easier to be sure,
I will find solace, be happy as before.
Now those contented hours I spent with you have gone forever
Dearest friend, I'll forget you never.

Joy Gray

Special Friend

I only have one good one
And she irritates me
When we are together.
Better on e-mail, then
Whether I'm moody or not
She doesn't know.

Sometimes we go on the phone
And an hour passes.
Why can't I talk without my glasses on?
She's the same.
Extravagant the way we get together
But it suits us.

She's coming up from Plymouth.
We're meeting at The Metropole that was.
All that way to see her sister
Who's coming down from Whitby.
We'll drink from proper cups
Not mugs by the computer.

Who sang 'They're either too young or too old'?
That's us. Stuck in the middle.
We put the world to rights on the Internet,
Yet when we meet next month
Eager voices will stifle in ageing heads,
And we will speak politely.

June Broomer

My Special Friend

What would I do
Without my friend
Always there to
Listen and advise
Though life has parted
Us in miles
The telephone
Is our friend
We ring each other
Week by week
To gather all the news
The miles disappear
We are together
Again
My wonderful friend

Eileen Kisby

How Can You Be Fifty?

How can you be fifty, when only yesterday
We were running next door to drag our mates out to play?
Then off we'd go for a spill or a thrill
Pedalling our scooters down 'Shaky Hand Hill'.

We'd be over the fields for a crafty smoke
Or in the Stoolball coach sharing crisps and a coke,
Or swimming in the river (crikey it was cold!)
But we'd have got away with it if someone hadn't told!

We strutted around in our kinky black boots
And drainpipe jeans (boy, we got some toots!)
We thought that we would be really cool
When we went up to the grammar school.

But the homework and rules just addled our brains
And then old Dr Beeching took away our trains!
We got detention at the drop of a hat
So we quickly said goodbye to all that.

We all got married and went our separate ways
And had a few kids to brighten up our days ~
Now you're back (and about time too!)
But how can you be fifty? That's too grown up for you!

Barbara Mackie

Good Times With Old Friends

I remember good times with old friends
When the conversation never flagged
And gloom wasn't given a chair;
Voices playing like instruments
Of a profane ensemble
Honouring the air with jokes and laughter;
That rarest beast of all, the friend,
Displayed for all to see and mimic
And enjoy, the seeming end of sadness;
The capability of not suspecting
Decline into indifference.

To make a pun, even what appals
Peters out, and thus are we consoled;
Anchored in my little garden
Communing with beauty
An old man talking to plants
In dereliction of some unknown duty,
Guardian of a shrine
That is only mine,
Unable to malinger.

Christopher Humble

My Very Special Friend

I have a friend, a very special friend
Who is always by my side
Always there to listen and a hand to lend
Good advice I do receive,
Special knowledge freely granted
This friend will not forsake me and my path will never leave.

I see Him in the first fine buds of spring
And also in those lovely birds that sing
I see Him in the roses of the month of June
And when the cuckoo changes tune.
Autumn fruits and grain show forth His love
And winter snows as lovely as the dove.

When I am weary or disheartened
I talk with Him and feel enlightened
Nothing is too small or too great for Him to undertake.
His love is deeper and much purer than the loveliest lake.
I know it's unconditional.
He will never, never let me go.

Friends may come and friends may go
But He is always there to guide and bless.
His grace and peace is wonderful to know
He sends His spirit in that lovely voice so low.
Without Him life would be so empty
My Lord, my confidant, my very special friend.

Georgina Johnston

Soulmate

Once in every lifetime you meet him,
The one who knows you oh so well!
Shares your joys, your worries, your sorrows,
Supports your pain, your Heaven, your Hell!

You know each other from a past existence,
Perhaps before the pre-earth life.
He loves, supports, is always with you,
Through every form of pain and strife.

Love of souls is interconnected,
At your root, your very core!
You can't imagine life without him,
Seeing him, you want him more!

He understands without you speaking,
Gives you love unconditionally.
He's your soulmate, then and now,
And you know he will always be.

Debbie Pawley

Ode To An Old Friend I Saw In Asda

Was that really *you* I saw today
With shades on under hair of hay?
You that was always such a flirt
Stood there in that awful skirt?

My God, but time's been terrible cruel
To leave you looking this uncool
Your devastation's quite complete ~
A peach all wrinkled by crows feet

Putty sags where tender flesh once gleamed ~
No longer a dish ~ just pudding too-well-steamed.
Wrecked and ruined in the 'Soap-Powder' aisle,
You were stripped of your beauty, bereft of all style.

Unable to face such destruction, I fled,
Beat a hasty retreat via 'Doughnuts and Bread'
Boy, am I thankful you didn't turn and see ~
Or you might have written this about me!

Velma Dixon

Is It True?

I stand here every night and day,
But now I will just walk away,
I can't stay here and wait any more,
So now I'm gonna say I'm sure,
I can't stay with you all my life,
Our love has been cut down the middle with that blazing knife,

I can't believe it's true,
I can't believe I'm leaving you,
I stand here every night,
But when I look you're nowhere in sight,
I feel like I'm losing my mind,
As a boyfriend you're supposed to be here by my side,

I can't believe it's true,
After all these years we're really through.

Karen Knowles

Space Reverie

Space reverie is feeling free
Is floating on a misty sea
A reverie of space are we
While dozing in the sun

Space reverie whisks you away
With Hermes hands and feet of clay
A reverie with you I stay
While sleeping we are one

Space reverie, you're mine at night
Though daybreak sees you on your flight
A reverie just out of sight
A dreamer on the run

Space reverie your task is through
You've done all that you had to do
In reverie I'll stay with you
At night our life's begun

Kate Chevalier

Ada

Someone like Ada
Someone so dear
Always there, always near.
You looked after me
By night, by day
And when I went on holiday.
Where I lived till I was five,
Until I went home to stay.

Then all my life I kept in touch
Went to visit those I love.
I saw them every Christmas Eve,
And through the years as well,
Sadly time takes those away
How much we would love
To see them today.

Peggy Oliver-Rayfield

Searching For Affirmation

I try not to think, to remember,
but the memories flood back.

In trying to forget
    I am simply calling
forth every recollection I have,

and I am unsure
    which hurts more.

I sometimes wonder
    if the absence of remembrance
would be less painful,
    as to fully realise
one thing you must
    recognise its opposite.

If anyone was to ask,
    I'd look away
and tell them,

'I miss her.'

Perhaps in the affirmation
    of my grief I will find
acceptance and justification,

perhaps my reactions
    to my mother's death
will cease to be so
    restricting and callous,
severing me from myself.

Perhaps I could learn to
    celebrate her life more
than I mourn her death,

and perhaps that
    would be my final hurdle.

If I could jump that,
perhaps I could attain
peace.

A life's journey
awaits.

Debra Frogley

Untitled

I've done a lot of travelling
And I've walked a lot of miles
I've even emigrated
I've laughed and cried,
Had lots of ups and downs
I've loved and lost a lot of people
But you've always been my trusted beacon
I've told you all my secrets
And my tales of woe
And at times I've been a pain I know
And with the world we live in
Full of greed and bad moral
For all you are and all I am
With you I will always be akin
They broke the mould when they made you
A lover, a husband and a dad
Without a doubt the best friend I ever had.

P K Lengyel

I Will Remember You

(Written for a friend who took his own life at 26)

When spring is here and tiny buds bloom on the trees
And little birds sing out their sweetest melodies,
Young branches swaying gently in the breeze
I will remember you for you are all of these.

For you so loved the woodland's solitude
Did often sit within her quiet repose,
You loved the bluebells and its briar rose
I will remember you for you were all of those.

I often think of times that once we shared
Of laughter and of tears when you were there,
Why was I blind to see, or hear your helpless plea,
I wonder did you know I really cared?

When nature's autumn colours start to fade
And forest leaves will lose their golden shade,
I will awake to see the morning dew
And feel your spirit near
I will remember you.

But spring will come again and birds will sing
And buds will burst forth woodland's sweet flowers,
And in my heart your friendship still will ring
Of all those years we spent those golden hours.

Eileen Boucher

For Love And Friendship

My Love and Friendship for you cannot be destroyed, or
fade into oblivion.
Just because we may not see each other for many a year,
for my love, lives forever in my heart.
Even should the time come and bring with it a great storm, my
love will bend with the winds, but not break, and when that
storm has
passed, the love and friendship, I have for you will remain,
unhurt, unmoved and ready to stand freely and say,

I am still here for you to see and I have remained steadfast here for
when you needed me again.

Joyce B Burton

My Sister ~ My Friend

My sister is the other half of me,
Loves me for myself not what I ought to be.
She picks me up when I am low
And even points the way to go.
She knows my thoughts, my hopes, my dreams
She even shares my harebrained schemes.
Though I'm the elder, it doesn't show
Because she keeps me on the go.
When I wish to borrow, I know she'll lend
'Cos she's my sister, my best friend.
When we're together, life's such fun
We laugh and talk, till day is done.
And even though we're far apart
She's right here with me ~
    Inside my heart.

J V Benson

Too Late

Dear George,
    Thought it time
I dropped you a line,
Hope this finds you keeping well;
You know you should get a phone
Now you are living alone,
We could have a real old chat,
Memories of when we were kids
Can you remember
The things we did?
Two more pages, now I've started.
Next week through my letterbox
The letter I wrote a week ago,
Across the envelope,
One word, *deceased!*

Arthur Pullen

Come Visit

It has been so long since I saw your face,
It seems like years, but the days do race.
How I miss your visits, our cups of tea
    and weekly chats.
Demi in the pram, so small, so sweet.
I suppose there is no more pram,
    just two little feet.
A mother and daughter's relationship is
    special, so cultivate and cherish it,
    it will last all your lives.
The time is close; you'll soon be here,
I can't wait to see you all especially little
    Demi dear.
So please hurry, although this place is
    upside down,
Believe me, it is still wonderful Cape Town.

Denise Swanepoel

No More

No more sun upon your face
No more kisses or your embrace
No more tears and no more pain
No more will I see you again
No more suffering
No more sadness
No more laughter
No hint of gladness
No more will I see your smile
Your telephone number I won't dial
No more yesterdays nor tomorrow
No more anger . . . only sorrow
No more walking in the park
No more stars shining in the dark
No more you on which to rely
No more goodbyes . . .
'Goodbye, goodbye'
No more!

I think of you often.

Lynn Thompson

We've Walked The Same Path

The things we have in common.
  Surprise us every day.
The paths we've walked through life.
  Coincide in many a way.

We found true love the second time.
  Our first born, they have been unjust.
One parent, each, have let us down.
  And friends, we found, we could not trust.

It's time to enjoy our new friendship.
  We've survived the good and the bad.
What they lost, we have gained.
  So no more tears, no more being sad.

And so, my friend, the time has come.
  To put away our fears.
We will still walk the same old path.
  Together . . . And no more tears.

Fiorella Shaw

My Best Friend

Another year, another day
And our friendship will always stay
My best friend you'll always be
When it was only you and me
Can you remember when we first met?
And that day I'll never regret
And you are only special to me
Because you're the best ever could be.

Marika Shaw (10)

Memories And Rosemary

I remember you when we were young, so very long ago.
For some time we took the path that both our feet could go.
Together we played our childhood games, and shared our life we two;
Those games we played are with me still, when I think of you.
Your life was far from easy, that's why you came to stay.
And you and I were like family, and still I feel today,
That the things we shared when we were young I'll remember
come what may.
In life we took our separate paths, careers to follow, families to rear;
But now and then our orbits crossed, the fates brought us near;
And now and then we'd reminisce about those days gone by.
Those memories we both share, through years that seem to fly;
And those very early memories return to us more frequently.
While things of moment, yesterday, escape
with frightening frequency.
Our childhood memories may be coloured, as the tinting of the rose,
Of the fun we shared, and the things we did,
but the truth within us grows.
Those links we forged when we were young,
memories of pleasure or pain;
With luck and retained faculties will always remain.
And when some years ago, we met yet again.
I heard you had been diagnosed with a tumour of the brain.
I remember when the doctor said you'd live to see the day
You'd take your grandchild for her first day at school,
and probably in this way,
He gave you that ray of hope, that's still working well today.
Of course you have your moments of apprehension and pain,
But through it all the little girl I knew shines out again;
And once, sometimes twice a week although we're far apart,
We pick up the telephone and have a heart to heart.
We reminisce, and with frequency more memories return;
We play our life all over, and perhaps from the past we learn.
But all in all I'd like to think it's been a life, the part of it we shared.
A time we still remember as, a time when someone cared.

Jean Rosemary Regan

The Harvest Of Life

If the tree shall be her first home,
with the branch her own rest room.
Then I shall be the small hand,
to release her from the tomb.

If the fruit shall be her body,
with the skin her own ball gown.
Then I shall be the young boy,
from the forest into the town.

Shall the flesh inside her silk skin,
and the guild be dear to me?
For I saw you smiling sweetly,
from your graceful orchard tree.

Shall the juice that runs so freely,
be rivers of wine for me?
For I plucked you down my darling,
from a rich and fruitful tree.

Will this peach be firm and healthy,
will her seed prolific be?
As, I've wandered through these orchards;
Please; not deceiving be.

Will the body rest in silence,
will the mind, not troubled be?
As, I've roamed for fourteen seasons;
Please; let this beauty be.

Can this, the final harvest,
lay this basket down to rest?
For the fruit, now for consuming,
the peel, the juice, the flesh!

For if the juice, a habit be;
and the flesh thereof; dependency.
This boy, shall live o' gracefully,
with an angel sincere; divinity.

Sean Grundy

Dear Cousin June

I have turned off the TV and come straight to the computer to write to you on your sad loss. Thank you for informing me, I am so upset for you. I wish to express deeply and sincerely my thoughts and feelings for the drama you are now going through. I am not a poet or literary person but send you this poem . . .

True love that lasts . . . in the end has to be lost
things taken for granted always bear a cost
together your partner and friend seemed forever
and now apart, with broken heart, it's time to untether

When young and fresh with complexion unlined
and hair strong and lush in the style of the time
we avoid thinking ahead of what must happen one day
and don't worry until it's time the reaper to pay

But you've worked at life and a good one too
your love has lasted all the way through
you have given new life and a daughter greeted
your time with Brian cannot be deleted

It's chin up for you, as you're the one that's left
you will need all your strength now being so bereft
a time to remember Brian's life and not his demise
difficult I'm sure and so very hard to realise

Time is the only healer for an ache such as yours
the more time passes, the more distant painful shores
Brian is in your heart and shall stay there forever
he hasn't left, he's waiting, until we're all together

With love from your cousin

Mel

Jack

Jack, you are my treasure,
My gem, my precious jewel.
I'd like to keep you locked away
But that would be so cruel.
Jack, you are my little star,
That twinkles in the night.
If someone tried to take you away,
They'd have to put up a fight.
You have a face of an angel,
A sweet and innocent one,
But I don't need these words,
To say 'I love you, son.'

V Linnett

The Trouble With My Nan

The trouble with my nan is she spoils me rotten
She's bought me so many things, some of them I've forgotten.
If my nan hears a joke that she thinks is funny,
She oinks like a pig and twitches like a bunny.

My nan is the greatest cook, she makes lovely shepherd pies.
But she can't work out the video,
No matter how hard she tries!

Whenever I am sad, lonely or in trouble,
She's always there to give me a kiss and a cuddle.

Chelsea Rowe (8)

Untitled

I hated the way you'd squeeze
A tube of toothpaste from the middle;
I hated the way you'd always leave
The toilet seat ~ bolt upright;
I hated the way you'd always pick
Those piggy little toes of yours;
But most of all, I hated
The nights you were not there at all.

I miss the scratchy feel of your beard,
The feel of hair upon my face;
I miss it now you can't scrub my back,
And I miss the hugs and cuddles too.
I miss the walks on fresh spring mornings,
And those out in the winter nights;
But most of all I miss
You, now you're not there at all.

I long to feel your beard and hair,
I long for hugs and cuddles too,
I long for those walks we used to have,
And to feel you scrub my back.
It's now, I even want, the half-
Squeezed tubes of toothpaste;
To see you pick your nails and say,
'Well shut your eyes or go away!'
I want you . . .
Now . . . you're not here at all.

S Z Colson

An Ode To My Friend

Like lightning in the traffic
A tornado in the tube
Escalators steps and stairs
Always on the move

I followed in her shadow
Not quite sure what to do
Always ever confident
She would see us through

Crown jewels, cathedrals
You name it we did it
Museums, art treasures
Never a minute

Ted Heath, Timothy West
And of course, Princess Di
Weren't they lucky to see us
As by chance we passed by

My only contribution
Was to get the food and drink
She sat there like a lady
Saying, 'Get just what you think.'

Betty Doveaston

Untitled

(For the best friend anyone could ever have)

He's not just a father or just a friend
He's someone who's promised to be there till the very end
He holds so much love in his heart
For us a heart that beats strong, a steadfast love
Overflowing with compassion and care
Waiting to heal and answer our prayers
His loving eyes gently watch
They see into the heart to touch
For even the most hardened heart
Cannot endure when God's love starts
His tender, loving hands will hold
All of your fears when you're out in the cold
He'll intently listen to all you say
And no matter what he will never turn away
He'll understand you when no-one else can
He'll feel what you're feeling no matter how sad
He'll whisper gently when you're asleep
His secrets into your heart to keep
For he wants you to know of His love for you
That runs so deep, so strong and so true
He holds out His hand and offers His peace
A chance for us to know what it is to be free
Why do we sadden Him and look so afar
Searching for answers to find who we are
We are God's children, who loves us so dearly
With all of His heart and all of His being.

Nicola Davies

My One True Friend

I've only ever had one friend,
On whom I really could depend.
He wasn't quite like me or you.
He had four legs, his name was Blue.

He'd come, I didn't need to call.
His face lit up, it said it all.
He'd read my mind, my thoughts he heard.
He spoke, but never said a word.

He wasn't here upon a whim.
He knew how much I needed him.
The bond was there for all to see.
I knew how much he needed me.

But sadly now, he's passed away.
I lost a faithful friend that day.
A part of me went with him too.
My mate, my pal, I miss you Blue.

James Sedgwick

My Mother

I searched for you in the river of stones
The Greta
Lifting out lavender, pink, and quartz,
Beautiful boulders,
Your favourite colours,
But you were not there.
Perhaps you'd gone up
To the stone circle, so up I went.
I waited for the moon to rise
Over Helvellyn
Your loveliest place,
But you were not there.
Had you gone back to Grasmere
Perhaps to hear about Keats and Wordsworth,
Your beautiful poets?
There was no sign of you there.
I climbed up Honister
Up the miners' path
And looked into Ennerdale
Buttermere and Loweswater,
Your headiest views
But you were not there.
I thought I'd found your gravestone
By Brocklebeck, where you'd watched me play
But there was no inscription on the standing stone
And I did not know how to make one.
In the end I searched for you in myself
And finally brought to the surface
Your courage
Your willpower
And your strength,
Yet only I know
Of your resurrection.

Wendy Zoula

A Love Lost

I remember your smile,
I remember your kiss,
I remember the warmth of your wonderful bliss.
Your talk of life,
Your views on love,
The sun, the rain, the sky up above . . .
But you died.

Together we planned,
Together we dreamed,
Together we wheeled and dealed and schemed,
Of running away,
On that hot summer's day,
In awe, was I, at the things you would say . . .
But you died.

I think of your face,
And our own special place,
The memories time can never erase.
Your soft olive skin,
The passion within,
My soul, it does ache just to see you again . . .
But you died.

Now I sit here alone,
Faced with the unknown,
And the bitter blow that life has shown.
You should be here,
Holding me near,
Being together year after year . . .
But you died.

Elizabeth Hopkinson

My Friend, Tyson

They always say that a dog is man's best friend,
Well with my dog, they were right, because his cuddles never end.

He is really daft, I must admit,
But he understands the basic stuff like sit.
He lays on the floor and goes to sleep,
And when I move, he opens one eye and takes a peep.
If he is ignored by a female dog,
You can't hear yourself think through his very loud sob.

At dinner time he scoffs it down his throat,
Then he goes and eats the grass as if he was a goat.
He comforts me when I am sad,
And loves me even when my mum is mad.

He's been with me since I was small,
And has grown with me, now I'm tall,
He wags his tail and it hits my head,
So much so, it was numb and dead.

But he is still my pal through thick and thin,
Even if he goes through my mum's bin.
And then he goes and runs away and I wonder where he's gone,
But when I finally find him, I shout over to him, *'Tyson!'*

Luke Barton (10½)

A Legacy!

(In memory of my Uncle Garry 1992)

He was generous, funny and kind,
He will always stick in your mind,
In body he's gone, in spirit he'll stay,
His loss is a price many shall pay,
He inspires us all,
And won't let us fall,
When life lets you down,
Fight back and don't frown,
Always look on the bright side of life,
It will help you through any trouble or strife.

'There is always a bright side, you just have to fight to find it.'

Shelley Burgess

Friends Forever

We lived and loved and grew together
I thought we'd be forever and ever
His life was long and full of fun
We shared good times and now we're done.

Whatever my mood, he was always there,
His loyalty was beyond compare.
He'd offer up a friendly paw
And cold wet nose to reassure!

My dear departed doggy friend
Was with me to the very end
And now he's gone I won't be blue
But glad to have had a friend so true.

Kay Vincent

To Carole ~ My Very Special Friend, I Thank You

For all the times I have laughed with you
And for all the times I have cried
For all the problems I have shared with you
And for staying by my side

For the 'boozy nights' I've had out with you
When I couldn't walk home straight
For making sure I got there OK
And telling hubby why I was late

For keeping the chips and chocolates away
When I was on a diet
For telling me to cook the proper way
To grill and never to fry it

For covering up when I do wrong
And never judging mistakes I make
For putting up with my stroppy moods
And not getting mad when I'm late

For accepting me for what I am
And never wanting me to be what I'm not
For forgiving me for upsetting you
And making sure it is soon forgot

For telling me when my hair is a mess
And my mascara has run down my face
For leaving me alone when I have a bad day
And for giving me my own space

For letting me talk about things I love most
When others might think I'm a bore
For sharing my sad times and giving advice
And saying 'that' s what friends are for'

For all these things my special friend
I will thank you my whole life through
For you're one in a million ~ please stay part of my world
'Cos it would never be the same without you

(Love Lesley, July 2001)

Lesley C Gash

Friendship

You took and you gave in times of my need,
You took our friendship and strengthened the seed.
When I hit rock bottom you dragged me up.
I thirsted for knowledge, you gave me the cup.

You gave me the sun when I shivered with cold,
You gave me my youth when my body felt old.
You held back the rain when my thoughts were dry
For the answers you gave when I didn't ask why.

When I marched into battle you sharpened my spear,
Destroyed my enmity, calmed my fear.
At the border to nowhere, the end of the line,
You told me that I'd got a lifeful of time.

When my life had shattered, you did not quit.
You broke down the fragments and forced them to fit.
When the weight of a country lay on my head,
You tied up the demons and shot them dead.

When I was enslaved by chains of doubt,
You melted the bonds, threw the guilt out.
The kindness you cradled with infinite care
Was the needle of sympathy mending the tear.

A single soul that's shared by two ~
A perfect description of me and you.
Friendship, like a plant, does grow;
The further on, the more we know.
Friend, my guide, philosopher ~
The path we walk is steady.
I do not have to search in you
For what I see already.

Elaine Tasker

To The memories Of Lost Souls

(This poem is dedicated to the memories of lost souls, now that cruel life was stolen away)

I've shed many tears of sorrow,
I've shed many tears of joy,
I recall many years of laughter
There will be nothing to destroy.
For in my heart there may be sorrow
But the images will never fade,
For in my mind they're long memories,
I will take them to the grave.
For in my childhood I gained
Long-time friendships of many family and friend,
But even with death so final,
I hold onto the thoughts that we shall meet again.
So onward journey brave warriors
To the dawn lights when we meet again,
For there may be sadness in my heart,
But the memories will always remain.

Steve Allen (AKA Sid)

Sleeping Through Life

I dreamed of you last night.
Didn't want to, but I did.
I slipped between my sheets,
And slid into the past.

Your eyes lit up with joy,
As I softly bit your lip.
A tingle down my spine,
As you whispered in my ear.

You smiled at me with love,
Not hiding true contempt.
We held each other's hearts,
Made love until we wept.

Collapsing in on one another,
As two became but one.
This dream of mine seems too real,
For just an audience of one.

Could it be, you share my dream,
Behind your mask of hate?
Do you rise each morning, cold,
Afraid of what's too late?

To catch what was and make it now,
From dreams into this world.
Until that day of fantasy,
In dreams I'll stay unfurled.

The ecstasy of love, in dreams,
A love that cannot die.
A love I visit every night,
A haven in my mind.

William J Bell

Smiler

Smiler ~
Where's your smile?
I haven't seen it for a while.
Fun lover ~
Where's the fun?
We're all too busy ~
Work to be done.
Cheeky ~
Where's your cheek?
You're all aloof,
A fashion freak!
Cool dude ~
Why be so cool?
Home is the place
To break those rules.
Sunshine ~
You're my sun
I need that sparkle,
It's my taste of fun.

Smiler ~
~ Give me a smile
Remind me how it feels just one more time!

Elizabeth A Green

Special Friend

Ever since I knew you,
You've shown me that you care,
You're someone really special to me,
As a friend you've always been there.

We've been there for each other,
Through the good times and the bad,
You've never let me down at all,
You're the best friend I could ever have.

There are not many friends like you,
Who would sit down and take the time,
To listen to what I've got to say,
To help get things off my mind.

No-one can ever mean as much to me,
As you do right now,
I've always wanted to tell you this,
But I think you know somehow.

When I felt so alone at times,
I thought there was no-one that cared,
But you seemed to understand,
And with you, my problems I shared.

Friendship is all about being there,
And never asking why,
I'm so happy you're a part of my life,
You help me get through every day.

I've never had anyone like you before,
Someone who's been a true mate,
When you came into my life,
I knew this had to be fate.

Emotionally you were there for me,
When I was feeling so weak,
You helped me through a difficult time,
That's what makes you so unique.

You'll always be a part of me,
Because of all the things we've shared,
I love you so much with all my heart,
You're the only one who's ever really cared.

Debbie South

My Tribute

A sorry sight he looked when we first met,
just skin and bones, a nervous wreck.
He gazed at me with eyes so sad
how could someone treat him so bad?
His head hung low his tail so still
the happiness he yearns I will fulfil.

I gave him my love and security
and in return he warmed to me.
The years rolled by and I gained his trust,
for a setter he didn't have the wanderlust.
But was fun-loving and bounced around
he was special and I felt ever so proud.

I remember that day at Egton Show
to all the dogs he wanted to say 'hello'.
Although he was busy sniffing at other pets
he collected a few 'placed' rosettes.
The obedience test was the highlight of the day,
for their dog to win, each owner did pray.

As I led him in the ring amidst the crowd
the entrants pointed and laughed aloud.
I stroked him proudly and made a fuss
and whispered in his ear: 'This is serious.'
He walked close at heel and followed my guidance
the crowd stared in amazed silence.

He proved to all that he was talented
when first prize was deservedly granted.
He can be a mischievous little clown
but he will never ever let me down.
He's faithful and true, a loving companion
and to me he is my very own champion.

Alas the years have now flown swiftly by
and to my faithful dog I had to say goodbye.
My heart was broken and my tears did flow
but he was old and tired so I had to let him go.
He proved to be a special and loyal friend
he deserved a dignified and peaceful end.

My ray of sunshine has been darkened by the pain
but my fondest memories will always remain.
Although we finally had to part
there will always be a special place in my heart.
In body he has left this life forever
but in spirit he will leave me never.

Anne K Byrnes

Together Forever

Slowly our friendship turns into love,
Everlasting days of laughter we both share.
Your friendly smile and caring eyes I adore,
You are so reassuring at every moment.
When you are away I think of you often,
A smile appears as my thoughts go on.
I feel I know everything about you,
You seem to know how to make me happy,
Every time I feel low I only have to look at you,
My tears and sorrow are turned into joy.
I have never felt so close to anyone,
No-one could compare to what you give.
I never want this happiness to end,
Always I want my life to be with you.

Zoe Fitzjohn

Remembering Kate

Remember how with joy I ran to meet you?
And how my being just sang and sang again?
The road that took me to the door of friendship.
Was just along a narrow country lane.
Forget not please the days of love and laughter,
When still I longed for hopeless, futile things,
Believing now that you're alive in spirit
You know the mystery that dying brings.

Amy E John

Sarah

Sarah never has a minute to spare,
Having a day out is quite rare,
But on Tuesdays, often it's a different matter,
Sarah allows herself out for a natter.

With her new handy address, and now living close by,
Sarah can easily take care of James, Josh and Guy,
Simon pops in for a snack and a talk
And all Monty needs is a good long walk.

There are only a few problems at Sarah's new abode,
Like transporting frogs over the road,
Don't waste time moving frogs in a bin,
You know they'll come back ~ you just won't win!
Painting walls and wardrobes ~ don't despair,
It doesn't matter if you've only 2 pairs of trousers left to wear!

Teaching art to the seniors at St David's School,
To her pupils ~ Mrs Smith-Williams is ~ simply ~ 'cool',
She's always busy in meetings and with school detail,
Oh, by the way ~ when is the next car boot sale?

Should you try to visit her at the apartment,
You'll find her at the new pad
You can never get her on either phone
It really drives her mates mad!
She'll have left already . . . for Ikea . . .
She's always there . . . and never here!

To Cornwall, Sarah and family often drive,
That's where Sarah likes to thrive,
On peace and quiet and cottage'y thing,
Whilst Simon occupies himself ~ sailing.

So the girls are off now on another jaunt,
To the Millerhowe Restaurant,
Up to the Lake District and through the hills,
We do hope Sarah's ingested her travel pills.

To Sarah ~ LTB (Lunch Time Babes) Resident Art Historian

Gillian M Hesketh

My Special Friend

You are my very special friend
And very dear to me
I love you with all my heart
And this is plain to see

No matter what is going on
You're always there for me
To reach out a helping hand
Or lend a shoulder, if need be

With troubles you always help me see
By guiding me along
You're always there to give advice
And help me to stay strong

We can talk and laugh together
And share a tear or two
We're never very far apart
Our differences are few

You're always there to give support
Which I'm willing to receive
You're showing you believe in me
And this helps me to achieve

You share in all my glory
And never have looked down
Even when you don't agree
You never wear a frown

You always have a smile for me
And I have one for you
We have a bond that's very strong
And a friendship that's quite true

You are my very special friend
Thank you for all you've done
You are my very special friend
You are of course my *mum*

J Preston

Happy Child

I remember a child, who when young
was fair, with hair like a waterfall
that gave hands the impulse to touch.
Her eyes were not blue, but grey
flecked with amber, large and bright.
A face that showed a happy nature,
full of character, it reflected every mood.
She walked into a room bringing sunshine
that had the magic to touch every face.
Laughter quietly filled sombre spaces
and music was dancing in the air.
I remember this child, the essence of happiness
who brought much pleasure, in many ways.
To relive these treasured memories
brings sweet magic to my declining years.

Dorothea Green

Goodbye

Goodbye my friends
I'm moving on
To pastures new
And far beyond

A new beginning
A new school
Making new friends
Making new rules

But keep in touch
Don't lose faith
I'll always write
Or phone in case

You need to ask
Or need to speak
Letting me know
Who's taken my place

Friends are forever
Friends are for keeps
So please stay in touch
Don't let me down please

Georgina Jackson (11)

For A Friend

Wow! Seventeen years old, a life ahead.
Fantasies and dreams, emotions to dread.

Suddenly a pain that changes a life,
Hits with fear like a sharp-bladed knife,
Why oh why do some suffer pain,
17 years old is no age to go insane,

A sudden change to look ahead,
Of scary fear that some have to dread,
Is therapy the only way,
To keep alive without no say,

Seventeen years old and a life ahead,
But days of feeling lethargic, that end up in bed,
The body is deteriorating and fading away,
We have no control and have no say,

Looking in the eye that shows the hidden cry,
Knowing that one day he is going to die,
We say to be strong, take time to feel tough,
But these words I'm afraid, are not enough,

The hair that falls out because of treatment,
Eyelashes go because of treatment,
One loss of confidence and self esteem,
Life can be so terribly mean,

So cherish the health that we have today,
Remember that some have no say,
Shattered dreams, some have to face,
Going through that terrible race,

Remember, the ones that have good health,
Because we have no clue,
What cancerous people go through,

So thank You God for being there,
And be with those and calm their fear,
One day they'll have no pain to fight,
Please be with them throughout the night,

Appreciate the life we have got now,
And cherish every second we have, but how?

Hannah Hubbard

Gordon

I like Gordon; he's the coolest man I know!
He's just so . . . so . . . himself!
Totally unpretentious, but a man who's been there!
Where! Oh every bloody where,
Glastonbury 1985, Yea!
He's lived with travelling people in tepees and tents,
Living his life and not paying rent.
Oh yes, Gordon's been there!

His house is such a mess,
But people go there under no stress,
Just relaxed, being with him,
He's got everything there!
Books, batteries, wires, speakers, computers, CDs,
Candles, posters, wicks, gadgets, sawdust and trees,
Yes in the house
But there's never a mouse!
The spiders eat them you see.

Gordon knows about most things
He's an intelligent man
Yet, he can sit roasting chestnuts on a conventional fan,
He looks at the sky with a passionate eye
Teaching you things you never thought to ask why,
He's approachable, cultured and funny,
But thinks it's his failing not to have money.
He's a sound, sought-after bloke
Appreciated by all sorts of folk,
Who value his knowledge and his space
'Cause we know he's at one, in his own place.

Adele C W Lane

Friends?

They are very important,
You can have a reliable one,
You can have a helpful friend,
It's really fun.

I have a friend called Natalie,
She's the greatest,
My friends and I call her Tilly,
It's the latest.

She helps me when I'm down,
And tries to cheer me up,
I like that very much,
She deserves a cup.

Natalie is always smiling,
Which makes me feel nice,
She's very squeaky,
Sounding like mice.

She's really weird,
But that's in a good way,
I find her funny
That's all I have to say.

Eve Lester

Mum ~ My Special Friend

Kindness, patience and judgement so fair
No other mother can compare
But if she were to go afar
My heart would ache for she's my star
My friend, my pal, my guiding light
Love and comfort when she hugs me tight
While life was sad, my dreams had died
She held my hand, gave me back my pride
To you, I say oh mother dear
In times of need please do not fear
For when it seems that no-one cares
Look over your shoulder . . .
I will be there.

Joanna Reilly

Uncle Roy

(27-12-19 to 10-03-00)

Jovial, joking, full of life
Cheeky remarks
Confident strides
Slick black hair
Talking about flowers
Knows more than most
More than anyone about
Flowers in the post

Appreciative of nature
Natural form
Walking in hills
Sailing and golf
Intelligent, witty, nothing's left
Watch what you say
A comment's picked and with deft
Subjects out, too late to get away!

Encouraging me
All support
You had a real interest
A friend to talk
I'll remember you with fondness
An inspiration in my life
If I could be half of that
Then that would be nice.

Mark Blackmore

Nanny

You were always there when I needed a friend
You took us on our holidays
As I get older I miss them.
You taught us to make good of the bad
When the sun shone the telly was banned.
I hold many special memories of picnics in the rain
And hailstone sarnies on the beach,
Ha, ha I laugh out loud
As I remember all the fun we've had
I know without you
Those images wouldn't have been so much fun
When I was much younger we would walk for hours,
I will treasure my memories forever
Because you made them so special
For you with love
Forever

Felicity Law

Odyssey

Friend ~ A person to be relied upon
Someone who stands beside you
Through thick and thin

You are this and more, much more
You're there when I need you ~ you care.

You don't solve things overnight
With your ideas we work it through
The end result is always right.

No mobile is needed, you're always near
Understanding forgiver ~ when I get it wrong
Gentle hug and then chase away all I fear.

You're a wizard at finance
To me bills are a worrying task
And winds me into a merry dance.

Accountant ~ philosopher ~ mentor ~ friend
Someone who always has spare time to listen
A true, true friend through to the very end.

David Charles

Friendship

Forty years of friendship
We've shared through the years.
Forty years of happiness,
Laughter and some tears.

Summer Fetes and Flower Shows,
Weddings in the sun,
Barbecues and holidays,
We've always had such fun.

Those far off days in Italy
How could we ever know?
That the bond formed in Cattolica
Would forever grow and grow.

May our futures long continue,
Our friendship forever be blessed,
With caring and with kindnesses,
With loyalty and trust.

Moya Charlton

To A Daughter

You, who as a child,
would not venture
beyond Deadmole Camp
cannot content yourself
with sitting on a hillock.
Some urgent driving force
speeds you across the world.
Face turned to the West
then to the East
Now North, now South
spreading your wings
till the feathers fly ~
and at each journey's end
there is but a return
to a central point.
Once more to fling yourself
into the turmoiled world.
The pot of gold is there
but no, you walk the rainbow's arc
to search its further end.
The pot of gold is here?
There is no pot of gold.
It is the expectancy
which gives the impetus
to your far flung journeys.

Joan R Gilmour

Hazel Eyes

Time was when I ~ a lonely guy,
Had lost my lifelong love.
There was no time to say goodbye,
She flew to heaven above;
And then one day ~ to my surprise,
The good Lord smiled on me.
He sent a girl with hazel eyes,
To love and comfort me.

She's gentle, kind, and caring too,
And Margaret is her name.
She seems to be saying 'I love you',
And somehow I feel the same;
Her voice it sings with pure delight,
In lilting Cambrian tone,
But when it's time to say 'goodnight',
Once more I'm so alone.

Sometimes I'm still a lonely guy,
When skies above are grey.
I say to myself, 'If only I
Could be with her today;
I'd give her tender loving care,
Through every night and day,
We all must have a dream somewhere,
And mine is here to stay.'

At sunset, and at sunrise,
And for eternity,
I dream about those hazel eyes,
And what they mean to me.
They speak of loving, caring,
And smile so tenderly;
I'm so proud to be sharing
One as beautiful as she!

J R Standeven

My Friend

My friend Terry was my best friend at school
we laughed together and played the fool.
She was always ready for tennis or games
and we went many miles cycling round the lanes.

When in our teens war broke out
so hard to believe what it was all about.
We lost touch for many days
having to go our separate ways.

When all was over and peace at last
we met up again and spoke of the past.
Things were never quite the same
so many changes ~ the war was to blame.

My friend married first and our friendship grew,
soon I moved away and was married too.
She became ill and died in a year,
her laughter again I will never hear.

She was my best friend of schoolday years
and when she passed on there were many tears.
Life goes on and we have to bear
the grief we feel when someone's not there.

Kay M Hook

My Mum, My Friend

My mum
    Carried me for nine months
I hope I came up to expectations and was trumps

My mum
    Nursed me through my first tender years
At times because of me mum shed many tears

My mum
    Comforted me through my childhood ailments
Through onto many teenage battlements

My mum
    Listened and tenderly loved me from head to toe
When I was a child of woe

The years roll on
But our memories have not gone

My mum
    Taught me correction
I still ask her to lead me in the right direction

For my mum
    I always find time to share
We joke and laugh
At many a story and old photograph
We realise how we have changed from yesteryear

For my mum
    I always try to have a strong shoulder
For her to lean on
Now that we are both older

M Wood

Lines To A Friend

Friend of many years I send
Love's greetings in hope today.
You'll not miss the time of year
When we two did plight love's troth
And in hope the future sought.
You'll not miss the time of year.

Friend of many years I send
Flowers on a scented page,
Just a wee forget-me-not.
May specious blooms our love supplant
In a rich soil evermore
Not far from passion's door
In a season sick with want.

Friend of love in hope today
Let these flowers on a page
Bloom within a throbbing heart,
A forgotten tryst its wage.

Angus Richmond

Heather And Ling

In my plant book 'quote',
Heather ~
a common, low growing evergreen shrub.
Common.
How could they call you common,
when next to the gloomy, dark corridors of cone-bearing pines
your flowers come alive, grace the earth with bloom.

In my plant book 'quote',
Ling ~
small pale pink flowers,
often seen next to Heather.
I thought,
so that's it.
During our neighbourhood years we grew together,
clothed the land in our garments of purple, pink, yellow,
the delicate throat of the siskin
singing out our friendship to all who wished to listen.

And now,
even though those neighbourhood years are no more
I can still hear your hushed bells whisper our rapport.

Sally Ann Ling

No Distance

The touch of an unseen hand
Holding me safe, secure
In the warmth of constant companionship.
Your welcome, always waiting for me
To come that we may be together.
Your generosity providing so much
I could not possibly aspire to.
Your endless understanding
Reassuring me when things go wrong.
Your tolerance to all,
A shining example to guide me.
Your voice that gladdens my heart
Always speaking with compassion.
Your eyes alight in merry twinkle,
You indicate life is for living joyfully.
Your kindness far reaching
Never leaving me short of help.
Your compassion so evident
In all that is said and done.
Your endless patience enduring life's trials,
A witness to believing in hope.
Your willingness to come into my life
And share the many ups and downs.
There in all events, circumstances
Of my every day. Not by mere chance,
But by choice. Inviting my heart to yield
That we may fuse together.
Travelling on as one inseparable,
Where love knows no distance.

Sue O'Donnell

Our Ton'

(From Tony, with love to Peggy)

Tony Dowdell to my husband was a lifelong friend, to me a special acquaintance right until his end,
Our son Anthony carries forward his name, as a symbol of what from Tony we gained,
Loyal, honest, trustworthy and giving, Tony was an extremely exceptional human being.

Every one loved 'Our Ton', he always smiled and never moaned,
His gorgeous grin, locks of white hair, his time to chat and ear for listening,
Are just a few of the things, we miss, now in heaven Tony is resting.

Tony was a simple man, with a heart of gold and a stature grand,
A string of talents his work will forever boast, the manager of our abode was his last post,
To the side of our house, Tony built his home, creating it inside his very own Dome.

He joined in a vision to ballroom dance, and upon meeting Peggy he took his chance,
Tony's beloved companion for many years, she made him laugh, smile and cheer,
When Tony's illness struck, she nursed him to sleep, wishing him eternal luck.

If he were here now I wonder what he'd say; 'Hey Jo, what a beautiful day'
'Give Peggy my love, a hug and a kiss, and tell Richard his stories I passionately miss'
'Anthony your adoring son, truly honours me, his naming, I still find quite hard to believe.'

If he were here now I wonder what I'd say; 'Hey Ton' are you having a nice day?'
'Peggy's doing well, your family too, Anthony, I and Richard dearly miss you'
'I bet you're having fun, watching over us, we all love you Ton' and look forward to catching up.'

J Dicks

You're In It For Life

Friendship, you're in it for the rest of your life
Even if you don't see your bosom friends for years
They are never forgotten.
Memories come back
Like polished sterling transformed
In time over and over again
When you least expect it
Life forms reappear
Images stand out
You wish them captured for an eternity
They will never be lost in a mist
But preserved and encased
So that, when their names are called,
They appear
Ready to sing, walk, dance or listen,
Or just be your friends again.

Nancy Treu Klotz

High Summer

We strolled together, she and I,
hand in hand, that summer,
wandered awhile on nature's pathway.
Our eyes were only for each other,
we had no glance to spare
for hedgerow, harebell, henbane;
our ears were unaware
of skylarks soaring, pouring high notes
from heaven down to earthly resonance ~
before modern monsters
swallowed corn and partridge,
corncrake and harvest mouse
without pause or patience.

We danced together, she and I,
breast to breast, that summer,
waltzed away the hours till midnight,
in harmony with nature's ways.
Enslaved, I could not slip my bonds
to roam beyond the beauty of her eyes,
sense the essence of her feelings,
engage her soul in locked embrace ~
until first love began to fade,
gently, with autumn leaves descending,
as love and life and all related things
must have an ending.

Andres Larchess

Remembering Friends

(Dedicated to an old school friend who was always with me in adversity, and has now gone beyond)

A good friend is the salt of the earth
Without which, life would be bare
A friend is one who knows the worst,
and knows the best
And who is with us always to share
All the sorrows and joys we go through,
As we pass along on life's great journey,
Until we halt at God's behest.

A friend is always nice and kind
And in such a one we can find
That in this world, we are not alone
A friend will never let us down
Always being there for us
Forever in pain and adversity
Bearing grief as though their own.

A friend is there when in need
One who will partake in
every little deed ~
Be it picnic, holiday or party
Always ready for one to turn to
Whatever we decide to do
One who will never hear one
word against you
If this be so, your fortune is in
To have a friend good and
true from within.

Blanche C Rice

In Memoriam CPH

My friend had served in India,
A parson's son, but game,
A tiger on the field of play,
A teacher he became.

Old school and strict but kind to those
Who lacked a cheery friend,
Instructor of the greatest skill,
He could at times unbend.

As for the boys within his care
He understood them well
And they responded ~ did their best ~
As he was proud to tell.

He had his eccentricities,
His special words of praise,
His heart was truly in his work.
To him my glass I raise.

Peter Spurgin

Remembered Friends

For many years I have faced the world alone,
Not caring about what has gone on around me.
But now as I stand on the peak of reality
I realise I want what I have once known.

As I start my search to the back of my mind,
I lower myself to the chair.
Finally I reach the end of my thoughts,
Not knowing what I would find there.

I lifted my eyes to the windowpane
And watched snowflakes fall from the sill.
I suddenly felt forgotten emotions
Which made the world stand still.

I remembered an image, clear in my head,
Of a girl that I had once known.
I recognised her from a dream,
A dream from long ago.

I recalled the momentary happiness
That we both had once shared.
The joy she brought when she smiled at me
And the grief she brought when she glared.

We had been the best of friends,
Nothing could keep us apart,
Until one day when fate had its way,
But she'll still be there in my heart.

Since then I've longed for a companion,
A friend as loyal as her.
I wish the joy was more frequent,
But nothing will occur.

Every night I wish upon a star,
In the hopes I'll be sent a friend from afar.
Even though my best friend is gone,
I know that our friendship will always live on.

Gemma King

Childhood Memories

I watch the shadows of the trees wave across the church,
The stained glass windows making them more elusive.
As I sit and listen to the sermon I let my mind wander
To childhood days when I was hypnotised by the sea
As Father steered our boat, the bow forcing its way through the rough waves,
Almost hearing the smash as we hit another wave, causing the boat to shiver.
When it was fairly calm the motion almost lulled me to sleep
But if a strong wind produced high, choppy waves
I had to concentrate, not wanting to fall overboard and shame myself.
So many stories would my mind conjure up while I sat
Balancing on the 'bench' formed from coiled ropes and sails.
Now whenever I'm near or upon the sea I muse upon her history.
As a child I was too young to realise that man abuses her,
Forcefully reclaiming land and wondering why disasters occur.
Her colour changes depending on the sky, her depth and the clarity.
We can see the fickle lady whose temper changes at whim,
One minute calm, the next an angry roaring tempest.
And her companion, the wind, only felt as he rustles by,
Causing the trees' shadows to wave across the church's windows
And stirring childhood memories.

Tilla B Smith

Gordon, My Dive Buddy In Ullswater

Lake Diving is not everybody's cup of tea.
The water is dark, forbidding, frightening.
An inky mass surrounds you
When you descend beyond twenty metres,
And you have to keep moving
As you dig in the mud for treasure.

Silt surrounds your head, and you have to rely on touch.
Your Buddy is your lifeline to sanity,
Hearing those bubbles,
Feeling the rhythmic kick of the fins.

Vision is restricted to the beam of your torch ~
No expense is spared!
A *vital* piece of equipment!

Thirty metres down is *serious*,
And *enormous* powers of self-control are needed at *forty*.
This is no place for the fainthearted or the Claustrophobic.
Narcosis, Blind terror Nightmares lurk here.
All the demons of the deep are waiting to trap the unwary.
A few minutes at depth digging for bottles,
And the controlled ascent begins.
Checking equipment, Sharing signals, Ascending.
Relief, survival, sunlight
In the final six metres.

What treasures are in my goody bag?
A broken Cod bottle, a stone ginger,
Pound coins from under the slit.

Another dive recorded.
Another signature from Gordon in my logbook.
Another battle won.
Nature at is most powerful defeated!
Coffee and Chips in the Hikers' bar with trusted friends
And lies told about how we all enjoyed it!

Doreen Hanley

You

I must get a life.
A life that's worth something,
Something that will pull me through,
Pull me through the thickest of problems,
Problems that floor me,
choke me,
gag me.

I must get a life.
A life that gives contentment,
Contentment in my soul;
My soul is emptied by lonely thoughts,
Lonely thoughts that flatten me,
drain me,
break me.

I must get a life.
A life that satisfies my needs,
My needs which start with you,
Start with you, continue and
end
with
you.

Kate Woodruff

Mum

Mum, when you were ill, you needed me so
You could cope, needed me to understand,
Because you were too scared to be alone,
And you needed me to hold your hand.

Mum, when you were dying, you needed me,
To comfort you and sit there by your side,
The pillar you could lean on, the love you
Could rely on, the one who never cried.

Mum, when you were gone, and I stood there alone,
Knocking at your door to say goodnight,
And then remembering, who was there for
Me, to tell *me* things would be alright?

Mum, when I grew up sad and all alone,
Missing you in ways I couldn't understand,
Mum, who was there to love me and help me cope,
Mum, who was there to hold *my* hand?

Sophie Horner (14)

Vital Friends

Are friends vital?
Maybe, maybe not!
Conclusion 'yes' that is my quest . . .

It is my guess . . .
Without those ties ~ leaves . . .
Life unprotected by big white lies.

Kiss and chase is fooling around.
Small in stature that is as maybe,
Friends we are, if only three.

Conscience unburdened, a problem halved.
Not too late to make amends,
To someone who was once a friend.

Candlelight creation lights up a room.
Soft music plays its part.
Love enters, Cupid's arrow, pierces the friendship's heart.

Real closeness grows, years at a time.
Perhaps sharing many in remorse.
Light that tunnel . . . darkness has taken its course.

Married friend to lover, the impression is there.
Emotions . . . grave situation arises.
A questioning soul, follows many disguises.

'With a little help from my friends,
The Beatles' line rings true.
An anthem in these words, real friends reach very few.

Are friends vital?
Yes, they are!
Solid friendship sustains, near or no matter how far.

Take my word and treat them true.
The rewards outweigh, the unknown and new.

Chrissie T

My Best Friend!

Bad news called me up one morning
the tone of voice gave me my warning.
A horrible accident took you in the early hours,
mourners now going to lay down flowers.
Surely there must be some mistake,
it couldn't be true baby, it's you!

When confirmed the news was true,
it struck my heart, it broke for you.
And my tears they did not heal,
in my dreams it wasn't real.
I felt injustice,
the world was wrong.
It's here with us where you belong!
We all love you and want you here
and hope so much you felt no fear.

The church was full, many had to stand,
not so surprising,
you're on high demand.

With every tear rolled the thought,
of all the joy and laughter you brought.
We all have our memories and moments with you,
in our hearts we'll keep them,
and always love you!

Casey B

Tina

Tina has a great wee hoose upon the Appin hillside
A hoose which has a great big field where diverse rescued creatures bide
Sometimes I drive right through the night to spend a week or more
I stay in a rented house, Tina stays next door
And as I switch the engine off and open up the boot
Tina's front door opens wide and Tina staggers oot
'Oh hello, is that you back doon
Here look at me still a ma goon
Well, we've had such awful weather
See you later ~ huv a blether.'
She has a cockerel named 'Chook' that thinks it's dawn at 2am
Well, okay ~ I do get back to sleep but Tina ~ buy the man a hen
And when Billy jumps the fence once more
And eats the flowers that grow next door
A noise emerges from her throat
'I'm going to kill that bloody goat!'
She has a fox she calls Wee Man and a cat that I call Fluffy
He was the King of Appin once but now he's looking scruffy
Her house is full of books, just books, there's books on every wall
A modern 'Lady of the Canyon' ~ better than them all
And when the day is at an end ~ I've finished my hill-walking
It's time to fetch the carry-oot ~ time to start the talking
I talk about my poetry, she talks about the sewage
That leaks out from her septic tank ~ the pipes all need renewage
And we blether well into the night
We drink the red and then the white
And between us put the world's wrongs right
Well the poll-tax is an awfa scam
Should I sell the car and get a van?
Do the Highlands need a five-year plan?

And who can understand a man . . .
And much, much more there is besides
And we laugh until we split our sides
I'd drive five hundred miles today
If it was possible to stay
For Tina knows just how I feel
To her a problem's 'just no real'
And I can understand her too
For every problem she's been through
We've been through it together
Yes, Tina is a great wee friend ~ I really miss the blether
And when I drive five hundred miles we laugh a lot together

Albany McGregor

Remembering Friends

When I was carefree, and in my teens
I met my first love, at the age of seventeen
So young, yet such a foolish heart
The way I let him just depart

The way we held hands, as we took a stroll
Surely those hours are still untold
I knew that love could never die
When my clouds were in the sky

He held me so close, yet an innocent love
Just like the cloudless skies above
When kissing me under the pale moonlight
As the stars twinkled, to give the light

I remember my first love of long ago
Why did my stubbornness let him go
I shall never know to this very day
Why I let him slip through my fingers, in such a way

When he came home on leave from the barracks square
He would knock on the door, always and be there
We held each other, as the world went by
I knew he loved me, and surely I

Oh, my first love, of those golden times
That teaches me how, to put this in rhyme
The memories that we spent together
While dancing around the buttercups, and clover

Oh, those lost years of the past
Maybe we will meet again, at last
Would he be wayward, wise or grey
Would we remember each other, on that day

Or, would we meet past the Heaven door
Would we remember those days before

Jean P Edwards McGovern

An Aria Of Equal Wisdom

He sits in the tree and sings
Sings in the fog and mist
Songs of his own
His hope that she will come

His is the only voice this dusk
But he is a concert
A duet, a sonata from the branch
And as I walk, I hear him
He makes me also want to sing

I am gladdened, lifted up.
There's hope!
He doesn't know what I know;
His is a different knowing
But he's more expert in the bird wing;
A repertoire of endless new renditions

And that's how I want to think;
I'm not smarter, I know *different* things.
And will tell them that in London
When I sing my poetry
And they don't want to listen.

I'll think of dusk, this ardent bird
The soloist pursuing love
Being who he is without permission
That little voice at dusk
His own perfection. He likes for me to listen.

Karen Eberhardt Shelton

To A Real Family Doctor

Dear Doctor G . . .

We are writing you this note
To let you know
Of all the folks
You'll always get our vote

We see you going out at night
A sickness call to keep
How glad we are that we're not you
'Cause we can get some sleep

You're always on the go, we know
Be it hail, snow or rain
How on earth you can stay free
Of tiredness of the brain

Sometimes the pills you give us
Can just get o'er our throat
Heaven help our insides 'cause
Those pills could sink a boat

Quite nonchalant you write a line
To get our medication
Like poison 'to us' it tastes
Why! That's premeditation

But where we'd be without you
We really hate to think
Certainly not healthy
Well! Hardly in the pink

I'm sure there's others join in
In wishing you all the best
For Christmas Day and New Year
We hope you get a *rest*

We hope you have a holiday
Till 1985
And come back fighting fit again
To keep us all alive.

From the 4 chemical solutions

Janetta Robertson

Uncle Edgar

You were my friend,
I wish you were here.
The kindest man in the world
To me
And I miss you so much.

I cried for two days when
They told me that
You'd fallen asleep,
Never
To wake again.

I planted a tree for you
In my garden.
A Japanese willow
Which bloomed last autumn.

The leaves fell in winter,
Grew again in spring.
You are not here
To see them.

I send you my love every night
With a kiss.
God bless you Uncle Edgar,
Sleep in peace.

Burbara Zoppi

I Have To Let You Go

(In memory of Mike)

The time has come to let you go
I cannot keep you here
I have to say a last goodbye
Yet these are the words I fear.

For if, indeed, I say farewell
Will you still stay with me?
Or will I find you fade away?
Don't say that's how it will be.

I know you do not speak to me,
Yet still your words I hear.
If I now finally let you go
Will your voice, too, disappear?

Without you, I am not whole
Merely one that makes two parts
To let you go I cannot bear
I still love you with all my heart.

Yet, if I truly loved you
I would surely let you go
To find the peace you always craved
I know it must be so.

And whilst I want to keep you close
I know this can never be.
So go, dear soul and rest in peace
My love is with you ~ eternally.

Sue Southgate

Sheba

(To Sheba for 12 wonderful years of companionship and love)

She came into our family,
Sharing her undying love.
Now she goes to live with God,
In His Heaven high above.

No more problems, aches or pains,
No crying out at night.
The presence of her company,
Always a welcome sight.

Our Black Lab left today,
On her journey home.
I know she will be alright,
And will not be alone.

And if some night we look,
At a star-filled sky above.
We will see our friend Sheba,
Still sharing her undying love.

Russell Bassett Stanley

though not a child, i was still young when you died . . .

though not a child
i was still young when you died
the memories on hand
short formed and shaky

mother to my mother
known as mary to others
you were born, lived and loved
in the land i call home

i'm never quite sure
just how well i knew you
what i always remember
is how much i want to

browned photos record
someone older than you
someone quiet, someone sad
someone colder than you

i return to those fields
behind the church of your absence
as a pilgrim without creed
from a land without flowers

by re-reading your name
i repair tears in my memories
replacing wonder with warmth
reunited at last

edi little

My Grandma And Grandpa Hudson

With tender love in the air
and sweet polish everywhere.
How my grandma made a fuss of me.
Whilst grandpa was at work missing,
we would both sit reminiscing.
Over a cream cake and a hot cup of tea.

Grandpa would come home,
with lots of love to condone.
And a big loving cuddle for me.
On the dark furniture bright,
the cheerful fire danced at night.
With grandma and grandpa I was happy.

I have never heard them curse
or in loud argument burst.
For they came from a noble upbringing.
With warm smiles on their faces,
and many old-fashioned graces.
Their love made me feel like singing.

If both of them you knew,
you would also love them too.
You would adore their quaint loving way.
When grandma and grandpa died,
how I sadly wept and cried.
Oh Lord! I dearly miss them today.

Joyce Dawn Willis

Remembering Friends

The best friend that I ever had
Was my dear little mum.
When she cooked my dinner
I ate up every crumb.
She always fed and clothed us well
Although we were so poor.
And in the war when strangers came
She never shut the door.
Neighbours, Dad, Uncle Bob,
Harry and Grandad too,
Me and sister Vera
To mention just a few.
She was a friend to everyone
When bombs were buzzing round
Getting up at 2am
And going underground.
She always made the food go round
Whoever might be there
And she had such a pretty face
With lovely curly hair.
When it came to peacetime
She was always there
With a lovely mum like that
I hadn't got a care.
Two years ago I lost her
Now she's up there with my Dad
One day I'll be with them
So why should I be sad.

Mary Crowhurst

Lost

Once we met, our world was set for a lifetime,
Each with the other complete.
Our lives full of sunshine, dreams, rainbows,
With no place for pain, hurt or deceit.
No chance of my ever losing you!

Once we used to talk of forever.
The end of time was our dearest, close friend.
The moments, hours, days filled with laughter,
And nights of total loving we'd spend.
It's not possible for me to lose you!

We invested so much in this love, life, home.
Each part chosen and shaped with care,
To create this world of perfection,
For you and I to share.
How could I ever lose you!

How and when did it happen, did you notice?
Were you more aware than I?
When did this love fail to blossom?
When did my heart break ~ and die?
Oh, the thought of losing you!

Now the floors ring hollow to my footsteps.
The rooms are silent, bleak and cold.
The dreams once so full of life and living,
Are now faded, worn, withered, old.
Could I really be losing you!?

I wish you could look me in the eyes once more,
Hold my hands and feel the warm blood beat.
Make clear the apologetic, mumbled words,
And still those restless, shuffling feet.
Now I *know* that I've lost you.

Julia Whale

Friends

(For Liz and Anne)

Friends come ~ friends go.
Friends stop to say hello!
They may be near ~
They may be far!
But I know you're always there.
Miles away ~ but just round the corner
I know you'll be here if I call you
You're more like a sister than a friend.
You'll always be there until the end.
You don't judge when I'm right or wrong
You're always there to help me along.
My friends may come ~ they may go!
But I know you'll always be there ~
Just to help me along ~
And say hello!

Norma Spillett

My Prayer

I wake in the morning, open one eye
Look through the window at the world passing by.
I have a good wash, then get me dressed
In me old-fashioned drawers and me good thermal vest.

Don't bother much with fashions or fads,
Just me trousers and jumper and downstairs I pads.
Get me some breakfast, piece of toast, cup of tea
Don't bother much, after all there's just me.

The rest of the day is completely free,
No-one to consider 'Just Me'.
At the end of the day I climb the stairs
To the Good Lord above, I offer these prayers.

May You in Your wisdom, mercy and grace,
Allow me *more* time in this wonderful place,
But if I should happen to go in the night
I'll make jolly sure I don't look a sight.

I'll put on clean undies, clean drawers and a vest
To the people who see me I'll sure look me best
But I pray you dear Lord, don't let them put me in shroud
To show off me bottom as I float o'er a cloud.

'Cos I do have me modesty, I do have me pride,
And there's certain parts of me I still want to hide.
I've got a nice nightie to which I've grown quite attached
It's just for a special occasion, it's got knickers to match.

And I hope I'm remembered when my time has come,
For me good sense of humour, *not* just a pain in the bum.
But I pray once again Lord, in Your mercy and grace
Will you allow me more time in this Wonderful Place.

Margaret Toft

Terry

I feel so very sad today ~
My favourite friend has gone away.
Up to Heaven she softly flew,
Within the light of the morning dew.

I feel so very sad that she has gone away,
No more we'll romp and tumble amongst the new-mown hay,
No more within the tractor, together we all will ride.
No more within the truck, she'll ever sit with pride.

She was my one and only, friend forever true.
Her memory I'll treasure, within my mind anew.
And when one day we meet, within that heavenly place,
I know we'll both have joy, each written o'er our face.

So until then dear Terry, a grave for you we've made,
Words 'Rest in Peace' upon a cross and flowers there we've laid.
I'll love you forever ~ and I know my Dad will too.
So wait for us in heaven, till we come and visit you.

E J Sherwood

Sometimes . . .

Sometimes when faced with a crisis
When unsure of the right path to take
When afraid to make a decision
So afraid to make a mistake
When lost in a Sea of Confusion
Adrift on a Tide of Despair
When the world is crashing around you
Then reach out, and you'll find me there
Sometimes we need someone to talk to
Or maybe just be close at hand
A shoulder you know you can lean on
Not to judge, but just understand
For often the answer you're seeking
Will all become clear in the end
Just believe in your own inner conscience
And the help and support of a Friend.

Stephanie M Bines

Keeping Score

You showed me a game
When we first met;
I kicked you the ball
You shielded your net.

You were much better
Quicker and agile.
I made you impress;
You made me smile.

I'd visit you often.
You'd sleep on my lap.
And when your friends left
I'd come for a chat.

You never complained
When I wasn't too fussed
With your affection,
Which was often too much.

The last time I saw you
I was too busy
To spend the time
And let you sit with me.

The next time I came
You'd gone forever
Hit by a car,
Never recovered.

So all the love
You selflessly gave me
I can never return.
In the next life, maybe.

Mark Follows

My Best Friend

I lost my best friend nearly four years ago
She was my Mother and I loved her so
We would go walking in sunshine and in rain
Oh how I wish we could be together again
She was always there for me night and day
And always knew the right things to say
If I had problems she would always understand
And say don't worry and then hold my hand.
I miss talking to her, and seeing her smile
I close my eyes and imagine her with me for a while
Oh why is the world so unfair?
Sometimes life is so hard to bare.
My Mother was my best friend
On her I knew I could depend
It seems like a lifetime since she was here
But mostly at night I still feel as if she is near.
Now all I have is memories of the times we shared
And it helps to know she always loved me and cared
So this poem is for my Mother who was my best friend
Some day I hope that we will be together again.

Eileen Kyte

Remembering Friends

(For Claire)

I have a friend! She is my mother.
She's not gone yet but belongs to another.
I remember her then on warm summer days,
Weeding the garden and hearing her saying,
'Sing with your heart, always be gay.'

Cuddling our babies, singing us songs.
Childhood memories, now are all gone.
Into her memory, memories we share,
Of our dear mother, for whom we all care.

Diseased by Alzheimer's, warmed by her love.
Into the canyon we look for her touch,
Waiting and watching, seeing not saying
When will we lose her
When we go sailing?

Over the mirrors of years floating fast
Into the caverns of dark, distant past
Seeking to please her, seeking to find
Memories to hold her, memories sublime,
That will keep her in touch with remembering friends
That will charge her and bind her in minds once again.

Mary-Lou Parker

Remember Me

As the mist comes down
like a shroud
on this November day,
remember me
as I lie beneath
this cold damp earth
for which I fought
and fell,
spilt blood.

My soul sings
and leaps with joy
for the freedom
I won from
this you gained.

Remember me
as I lie here
beneath this foreign soil,
my spirit, imprisoned
yearns for home and
screams out loud ~
my England, my home.

Remember me
not with thanks nor
gratitude but with
a promise of remembrance
of why I'm here.

Kath Gabbitas

Happy Returns

Glimpsed from beyond the corner of my eye.
A move of changing light upon the wall.
Darker or lighter it shifts from left to right.
Someone is here, reminding me of all
That is not forgotten, whispering 'We do not die.'

Memories of those who left are never far away.
Not always in the conscious mind
But ebbing and flowing from day to day
Upon a tide fed by a waterfall of tears.
Flooding in, then washed away
Like sandy footprints that were left behind.
Then suddenly a presence reappears,
Replays the shadow show of distant years.

Essence of a loving friendship lingers on
To fill the gaps of all I lost and miss.
What would I give for one more smile or kiss
And gentle murmurs, echoing like footsteps long since gone.

One day maybe I'll tiptoe back
To be a shifting light upon the wall
Of those I love the best of all.
And filter through their thoughts, to say
'I'm here, almost within your sight.
For old times sake, and though I cannot stay,
Think kindly of your uninvited guest.'

Kathleen Aust

My Pal Val

(Dedicated to Val Parsons)

I have a friend
Her name is Val
For years and years
She has been my pal.

We worked and laughed together
Both liked to play cards
At lunch time, in the canteen
For the time to pass,

Now we spend
Our time on the phone
To Bristol Val has returned
That is her home,

We are very alike
In what we enjoy
Like food, Scrabble, puzzles and books
Or having a smoke
On which we are both hooked,

This friendship I know
Right through to the end
I'm lucky to have Val
A wonderful friend.

Irene Pierce

To My Friends

If you see a star out there somewhere
That winks the night through
It will be me as happy as can be
Sending my thoughts to you
This life now gone to a peace we all yearn
As you all have been with me
At each twist and turn
How can I thank you all so?
That you know how much you mean to me
Remember me
All those that saw me as I was, and held me
To those who walked with me
And wanted to hold my hand
I send you all my love;
Hold me gently within your minds
So that I may live forever
Remember the happiness of a young boy
With new toys
Also of the maidens that know
They are loved so.
This we shared
To you that hold me in your arms
I can feel these things
Through darkened days
I thank you for your lovely ways, and calm outsides
The turmoil deep, deep inside us all, is now shared
As we belong to all, and evermore will be there.
Forever friends

Yenti

Golden Memories

Him, I could never, ever forget,
    No longer to see, but remember him yet.
Even today, how I miss him so much,
    His laughter, and his caring touch.

As a baby he, did cradle me,
    Growing up, gave me *such* glee.
With him I would go, down to the farm,
    Where he would see, I came to no harm.

Walking the fields, so full of pep,
    Followed by closely, our sheepdog ~ Shep.
Watching the ewes in lambing season,
    To their lambs, life had a reason.

When told that he was coming home late,
    Down the garden path, I'd eagerly wait.
Someone passing said, 'It won't be long till,
    He comes down the road, our friend Bill.'

Although these memories are, of long ago,
    How much I *still* miss, and love him so.
Many happy memories my life has had,
    Given with the love of, my precious dad.

June F Allum

Old Friends

(For Tom)

In green fields let me run again and feel the sun upon my brow,
and let us be as one again, not far apart, as we are now.
Then let the joy course through my blood and let the bubbling
laughter rise . . .
let youth's first spring renew my blood and see the world through
wondering eyes.

Our skies were always blue my friend, the winds of life were always
warm . . .
of time itself there was no end: our ships could weather every
storm . . .
the hours we spent are not forgot, engraved in mem'ry they shall be,
for friendship was our blessed lot, and shall be for eternity.

That wide-faced, knowing, cocky grin, that questioning but
impish look
that seemed to take the whole world in, with life itself the
open book.
We trod the fields, we walked the lanes, we shared the lows and then
the highs,
we had our losses, and our gains ~ thus strengthened we our
close-bound ties.

There is no real tomorrow then, for slowly night pales into day . . .
and then we find 'remember when' is only just a thought away.
And so the numbered years have passed, for Time's not one to drag
his feet ~
yet soon or late, 'twill come at last, when once more two old
friends will meet.

Ken Allen

Margaret

That summer and the next
I was sent to visit an aunt.
It was not an easy journey
Two changes of trains
And a bus from Dowlais Top.

Looking back
I see my cousin Margaret
Like a series of snapshots
That never seem to fade.
Wading through the river near Sirhowy
With me, in totally inadequate shoes
Hopping from stone to stone.

We had planned a picnic
At the place they called Nine Arches.
I was never so happy.

Suddenly my mother came to take me home
Quite unexpectedly
We were to go to the seaside
For the rest of the holiday
Pleading was useless
It was all arranged.

Later they told me
I was sitting on the train
Not making a sound
But on my cheeks the most enormous tears.

Three weeks?
Not much in a lifetime.

But I remember Margaret
Wading through the Sirhowy river
Always nine years old.

Enid G Smith-Masters

Huckle

Huckle was my beano pal,
The scuff and nonsense we all went through.
A sort of Rod Stewart mate, a feather-cut,
Crombie-straight sort of mate,
And of course you love him
Because you manage magic when you meet,

He named all mum's beansticks Dimworthy and Coach,
Wrote stories called Stephen's Eggs
And Stephen's Dressing-gown Has Legs.
First I ever knew who came to school in segs.

He was a darkroom of scent,
We went through armpits of sweat,
Of Atom Heart Mother, Deep Purple in Rock.
We stayed awake through our teenage of shock
And Rothmans, and college, and dockyard . . .

That friendship is there like history at the door
Floating as a strand across old muddy waters;
Transparent from its infant source,
And wisely ~ we never disturb it.

Simon Carter

Nan

(Inspired because my Nan was my best friend)

I miss you Nan
Three years have passed
Though the pain numbs
My love is still strong
My thoughts to you I often send.

You had the wisdom
To know when to say something
The hug to comfort
The kiss to heal
The love always constant.

I close my eyes, I think of you
I feel your warmth embrace me
Lily of the Valley your special smell
I hear you chuckle
I sense you by me.

It's good to know Nan
That even in death you are with me
Picking me up when I fall
Guiding, reassuring me
But most of all, loving me.

Sue Presley

Friendship

I look fondly on our friendship,
And see a budding rose.
Its petals spreading gently.
A poem of beauty to compose.

It stretches forth its gentle hand.
Embracing rain and shine.
An offer to sip its nectar,
Tasting like the richest wine.

But sometimes offered only tears,
And fed with vile untruths.
Kills the rose of friendship,
Right to its very roots.

So friendship, frail and delicate,
Fear not this death from me.
I cherish thee more dearly.
For thou were meant to be.

Vincent Alexander

Recollections

(Dedicated to my Granda, Jack, who made life magical)

After you died,
we sat around. Once the tears stopped
I curled up in the leather chair.
The stillness was cracked
by someone talking in the other world
beyond your hospital room.

Something came over me
waves of shivering fear.
I started to laugh. Everyone's eyes bore
into me, drilling disapproval.
All I could do was blurt out
what I was recalling.
All the times you made life,
bearable.

Linda M Adams

Love Pained

He was her man with no name,
Above everyone else
He'd ever met or would,
He'd love her
Without feeling of guilt or shame.
For she was like an angel,
And he felt he was lucky
That into his life
She came.
And if other women
Thought he had a look
In his eye for them
They would be mistaken,
His quick on the draw
Answer being:-
'Sorry Ma'am,
My love . . .
Is already taken.'

She wasn't
And she was
His woman just the same
Even though over her
Another man had some claim.
They'd both drifted through life
Not knowing its greater scheme,
Only together
Finding they shared
Each other's dream.

Malcolm Peter Mansfield

Missing You

I had a friend, who was very dear,
 Sadly, he's not here today.
He was a friend I could love and trust
 Until he was called away.

I met him when I was only sixteen.
 An Airman, in Air Force blue.
We talked of events that where happening then
 And of the friends that he knew.

Soon he was posted to learn a trade
 To service engines in planes.
He loved that work. It was his life
 Using his skills, and his brain.

We corresponded, just as friends.
 His letters were full of good cheer.
He came to see me when he was on leave,
 That is when Love began to appear.

He was such a very good man.
 I admired him in every way.
He saw everyone's points of view
 And listened to what they had to say.

He made friends very easily.
 He would laugh, and joke, with the rest.
Whatever he was asked to do
 He did it, for the best.

Eventually, we were married
 Although we never made our Golden Day.
I wish I'd been with him, that final night
 There was still so much to say.

He was my Husband, my friend, and my pal.
    I miss him more every day.
He was too ill to wish he was here right now,
    But I'll Love, and admire him, always.

Joan Smith

Candy ~ A Tribute

Candy my joy, the love of my life
a cross Golden Labrador full of joy and light,
she was so intelligent she read my thoughts
and knew before me when my mind was so fraught.

At 6 weeks old she came into my life, full of joy and love,
surely a gift from God above.
Our bond was strong and disabled I might be,
Candy became my Aid and special to me.

She pulled me up mountains in the Cairngorms
choosing which steps she knew were the norm.
In 2001 on your birthday in May
we had to take you to the Vet for an X-ray.

At 13 years the Bone Tumour came, life would never be the same again
there would not be a life much more for my Wonderful Golden Labrador.
The news brought shock to everyone, but in human terms you are 91,
all too soon you would be no more, my Beautiful Golden Labrador.

I cried until I could cry no more, we tried to carry on as before,
you seemed to understand you had Arthritis, living with this you were the brightest.
You took all your medicine with delight, you greeted each day full of might,
what wonderful food you could get from me was taken or snubbed with impunity.

By now my life revolves around you, according just to what you can do.
My tears flow freely during the night, when you are safely out of sight.
When my Menieres illness was coming on, she did not hide,
her warning was clear when she would not leave my side.
My Disabled Aid, my Beautiful Maid, my Wonderful Guide, my Joy and my Pride,
how can I go on as before, without my Beautiful Labrador.

Mary E Cowburn & George A Cowburn